SPORTS TOP TENS

SANDY DONOVAN

Lerner Publications Company • Minneapolis

Lerner Publications Company
A division of Lerner Publishing Group, Inc.
241 First Avenue North
Minneapolis, MN 55401 USA

For reading levels and more information, look up this title at www.lernerbooks.com.

Library of Congress Cataloging-in-Publication Data

Donovan, Sandra, 1967–
    Sports top tens / by Sandy Donovan.
        pages   cm. — (Entertainment's top 10)
    Includes index.
    ISBN 978–1–4677–3842–2 (lib. bdg. : alk. paper)
    ISBN 978–1–4677–4676–2 (eBook)
  1. Sports records—Juvenile literature. I. Title.
  GV741.D66 2015
  796.02'1—dc23   2013042051

Manufactured in the United States of America
1 – VI – 7/15/14

TABLE OF CONTENTS

INTRODUCTION

Have you ever been blown away by an athlete's ability? Maybe you're following that pro basketball player who never seems to miss. Or maybe it's the superfast runner who leaves the other racers in the dust. No matter what the sport, there's something about truly extraordinary athletes that makes us want to keep watching. Sometimes those athletes inspire us to get out there and give it a try too. Other times, they inspire us to make lists of who's the greatest.

Wondering who's run the fastest, sunk the most baskets, or snagged the most Olympic medals? We've ranked some of the world's greatest sports icons in five mind-boggling top 10 lists. Each list is based on facts, such as performance stats or number of awards. Turn the page to discover some of the world's most outstanding athletes.

What athletic achievements make
Tom Brady so extraordinary?
Read on to find out!

TOP 10 OLYMPIC GOLD MEDALISTS

How do you decide who are the best Olympic athletes of all time? For this list, we've ranked athletes based on the number of gold medals they won. And then, since five athletes won eight gold medals each and four athletes won nine each, we've used silver medal wins and bronze medal wins as tiebreakers. Believe it or not, that still leaves two ties!

10. Matt Biondi: 8 gold, 2 silver, 1 bronze

US swimmer Biondi, a native Californian, racked up his impressive medal count at the 1984, 1988, and 1992 Olympic Games. In all, he set seven individual world records. Three were in the 50-meter freestyle, and four were in the 100-meter freestyle. Since retiring after the '92 Games, he's kept busy as a middle school math teacher and swim coach.

9. and 8. (tie)
Jenny Thompson: 8 gold, 3 silver, 1 bronze

Thompson's medals came from four Olympic Games: 1992, 1996, 2000, and 2004. The US swimmer from New Hampshire began swimming at the age of seven. At 19 she won her first two Olympic gold medals in 1992. After her days in the pool ended, she became a physician.

The butterfly stroke was one of Jenny Thompson's specialties. She showed off her strokes at the 1996 Olympics, where she helped win three medals for Team USA.

Sawao Kato: >>>
8 gold, 3 silver,
1 bronze

Kato was a leader of the male Japanese gymnastics teams that dominated the Olympics at the 1968, 1972, and 1976 Summer Games. He has more Olympic gold medals than any other male gymnast or any other Japanese Olympian. He went on to be a professor at Japan's University of Tsukuba.

7. and 6. (tie)
Birgit Fischer: 8 gold, 4 silver, 0 bronze

This German canoeist won her eight medals at six different Olympic Games between 1980 and 2004. In 1980 and 1988, she represented the nation of East Germany. In between, she missed the 1984 Summer Games when her country boycotted the Olympics for political reasons. A few years later, though, East Germany and West Germany became a single country after decades of separation. Fischer swam for a reunified Germany at the 1992, 1996, 2000, and 2004 Summer Games.

Bjørn Dæhlie: 8 gold, 4 silver, 0 bronze

This Norwegian cross-country skier is the most awarded Winter Olympian of all time. He dominated the 1992, 1994, and 1998 Winter Games. He was training for the 2002 Olympics when a roller skiing accident ended his career. Since then he's remained famous in Norway as a businessperson and philanthropist.

Carl Lewis nailed the long jump at the 1988 US Olympic track-and-field trials. He went on to wow judges and fans at that year's Summer Games.

5. Carl Lewis: 9 gold, 1 silver, 0 bronze

As a US sprinter and long jumper, Lewis has set his share of records. He topped the world rankings in the 100-meter, 200-meter, and long jump events throughout the 1980s and the 1990s. He built up an impressive collection of gold medals at the 1984, 1988, 1992, and 1996 Olympics. And his fame stretched beyond the track. In 1984 both the NBA and the NFL tried to draft him!

4. Mark Spitz: 9 gold, 1 silver, 1 bronze

When US swimmer Spitz won seven gold medals at the 1972 Olympic Games, he also set the record for most golds at a single Olympics. (That is, until Michael Phelps came along and won eight golds at the 2008 Olympics.) Spitz was only 22 when he retired from swimming after the 1972 Games. Since then he's been an actor, sports commentator, and real estate executive.

3. Paavo Nurmi: 9 gold, 3 silver, 0 bronze

In the 1920s, this runner from Finland dominated distance running. Nicknamed the Flying Finn, he won three gold medals and a silver medal at the 1920 Olympics, five golds at the 1924 Games, and one gold and two silvers at the 1928 Games. Specializing in middle- and long-distance running, Nurmi introduced the idea of "steady pace" training, which focuses on endurance instead of speed. Runners still use this method to get in racing shape.

2. Larisa Latynina:
9 gold, 5 silver, 4 bronze

Latynina collected 18 medals as a gymnast for the Soviet Union between 1956 and 1964. For nearly 50 years, from 1964 until 2012, she held the record for having the most Olympic medals of all time. She's still the only female athlete to have ever held that record—and she also holds the record for gold medals won by a female athlete.

1. Michael Phelps:
18 gold, 2 silver, 2 bronze (22 total medals)

At each of the three Olympics he attended, this US swimmer captured more medals than any other competing athlete. That's six golds and two bronzes in 2004, eight golds in 2008, and four gold and two silvers in 2012. Add them all up, and you have the most decorated Olympic athlete of all time.

Michael Phelps basked in his Olympic glory after a medal ceremony at the 2012 Summer Games.

HIGHEST SCORERS IN THE WNBA

Ever since the Women's National Basketball Association was formed in 1997, professional female basketball players have been tearing up the hoops. Check out this list to see which players have the highest average points per game in their careers:

10. and 9. (tie)
Tina Charles:
17.3 points per game
Since 2010, when she was the Connecticut Sun's No. 1 draft pick, Charles has proved she belongs among the WNBA elites. The evidence includes her selection as the 2010 Rookie of the Year and her capture of the 2012 WNBA MVP award. Still not convinced? She's also the first player in league history to record three 20-point, 20-rebound games.

Lisa Leslie: >>>
17.3 points per game
In 11 seasons with the Los Angeles Sparks (1997–2006 and 2008–2009), Leslie established herself as a dominant WNBA player. This three-time league MVP and four-time Olympic gold medal winner was also the first player to ever dunk in a WNBA game.

8. Candace Parker:
17.4 points per game
Parker has been a key player for the Los Angeles Sparks since she joined them as the No. 1 draft pick in 2008. The same year she was the first player in the WNBA to be named both Rookie of the Year and league MVP in the same season. Parker won an Olympic gold medal with the US women's basketball team.

7. Elena Delle Donne: 18.1 points per game

Before being drafted by the Chicago Sky in 2013, Donne was a standout NCAA player at the University of Delaware. While at UD, she became the NCAA's fifth-leading scorer of all time. After being selected second overall in the 2013 draft, she quickly proved her professional value. She helped the Sky qualify for the playoffs for the first time in the team's history—and earned herself the 2013 Rookie of the Year award.

6. Seimone Augustus: 18.7 points per game

Forward guard Augustus has never let anything get between her and the game she loves. At the age of three, she joined a basketball team for five-year-old boys. She's been on a roll ever since. In 2006, her first season with the Minnesota Lynx, she picked up the Rookie of the Year award. She was a league all-star in 2006, 2007, and 2011. She helped her team win the 2011 WNBA Finals, and she earned the WNBA Finals MVP award.

5. Lauren Jackson: 18.9 points per game

This Australian forward-center started playing basketball when she was four years old. The years of effort paid off. Jackson was just the third international player to be selected first overall in a WNBA draft. The Seattle Storm snapped her up in 2001. Since then she's been to eight all-star games and been chosen as the WNBA MVP three times (2003, 2007, and 2010).

4. Cappie Pondexter: 19.2 points per game

In her four years with the Phoenix Mercury (2006–2009), this all-star guard helped lead her team to two WNBA championship titles (2007 and 2009). Since 2010 she's played for the New York Liberty, with a total of five career playoff appearances and four all-star game appearances. In 2011, fans ranked her among the WNBA's all-time top 15 players.

3. Angel McCoughtry: >>> 19.5 points per game

McCoughtry *(player with the basketball)* was chosen by the Atlanta Dream as 2009's No. 1 overall draft pick. The standout guard and forward was named WNBA Rookie of the Year that season. At the 2010 WNBA Finals, she set the league record for most points, with 35 in one game, only to break her own record the next year with 38 points in a WNBA Finals game. In 2012 she led the league in steals.

2. Diana Taurasi: 20.6 points per game

This two-time WNBA champion (2007 and 2009) has played guard for the Phoenix Mercury since 2006. That year she was the youngest member of the gold medal-winning US Women's National Team in the Olympics. She went on to help the United States win gold in the 2008 and 2012 Games. In the WNBA, she's been selected for the all-star team five times.

1. Cynthia Cooper-Dyke:
V 21.0 points per game

This Houston Comets guard dominated the WNBA in its early years. She played for Houston from 1997 to 2000 and again in 2003. She's won championships in college, the WNBA, and the Olympics. In April 2013, she was named women's basketball head coach at the University of Southern California.

There are about as many ways to rank swimmers as there are types of swimming strokes. Here, we've listed the world's fastest swimmers, based on recorded times for the 50-meter freestyle. In this race, swimmers use strokes of their choice to race across the length of an Olympic-sized pool. The times below were all recorded by FINA (the Fédération Internationale de Natation, or International Swimming Federation). FINA is the organization in charge of international swimming competitions.

<<< **10.** Cullen Jones: 21.40 seconds

The US swimmer posted this record on July 26, 2009, at the FINA World Championship. He began swimming lessons at the age of five, after he almost drowned on a water ride at an amusement park! Today, he's part of the Make a Splash swimming program, which encourages children to learn to swim.

9. Florent Manaudou: 21.34 seconds

When Manaudou set this record, he also took home the gold medal for France at the 2012 Olympics. The victory made 20-year-old Florent and his older sister Laure the first siblings to win Olympic medals in swimming. (She won the women's 400-meter freestyle at the 2004 Olympics.)

8. Duje Draganja: 21.29 seconds

This swimmer from Croatia won the silver medal in the men's 50-meter freestyle with a time of 21.94 seconds at the 2004 Olympics. But he set his record time five years later at the 2009 FINA World Championships in Rome. From 2001 to 2005, Draganja attended school and swam at the University of California, Berkeley.

7. Eamon Sullivan: 21.28 seconds

This Australian swimmer posted his record at the March 2008 Australian Olympic Trials. He also held the world record for fastest 100-meter freestyle from August 2008 until July of the next year. Meanwhile, he scored three medals—two silvers and a bronze—at the 2008 Olympics in Beijing. But swimming isn't his only love. He's also an amateur chef and a proud restaurant owner.

6. Amaury Leveaux: 21.25 seconds

After winning two silver medals for France at the 2008 Olympics, Leveaux earned this record at the 2009 FINA World Championships. But after that, he failed to make a mark for the next two years. As he told one magazine, he'd been eating too much junk food. He changed his ways, got back in shape, and qualified for the 2012 London Olympics. There he helped his team snag gold in the 100-meter freestyle relay and silver in the 200-meter freestyle relay.

French swimmer Amaury Leveaux, shown here at the French swimming championships in 2010, announced his retirement in 2013.

5. Alain Bernard: 21.23 seconds

Bernard set this record at the 2009 French Nationals. But he's also known as one of the world's fastest 100-meter freestylers. He won gold in that event at the 2008 Olympics, becoming just the second Frenchman ever to earn an Olympic gold medal in swimming. (The previous win for a French male was in 1952!) In the 2012 Olympics, he helped his team bring home the gold for the 4×100-meter relay.

4. George Bovell: 21.20 seconds

Bovell, from the tiny Caribbean island nation of Trinidad and Tobago, has been to the Olympics four times (2000, 2004, 2008, and 2012). His 2004 bronze medal in the men's 200 individual medley (IM) was his country's first medal in swimming. He earned his spot on this list at 2009's FINA World Championships.

3. Ashley Callus: 21.19 seconds

Callus won his first gold medal on the Australian 4×100-meter freestyle relay team in the 2000 Olympics. But a virus knocked him out of the running at the 2004 Olympics. He was back on the winner's podium in 2008 when the Australian relay team won the bronze medal. In November 2009, he earned his spot on this list at the AIS (Australian Institute of Sport) International. Though he only held the record for a month, he remained a giant in the swimming world until his 2012 retirement.

Ashley Callus (front left) helped Team Australia bring home the gold for the men's 4×100-meter medley relay at 2006's FINA World Short Course Swimming Championships.

2. Fred Bousquet: 20.94 seconds

Is it beginning to seem as though there are a lot of French swimmers on this list? It's true! With four swimmers near the top of the heap, France has more 50-meter record holders than any other country! Bousquet earned the No. 1 spot at the 2009 French Championships and held on to it until the following year.

1. César Cielo: v 20.91 seconds

v
v
v
v
v
v
v
v

Ever think that 0.3 of a second could mean much? For César Cielo, that's all it took to nab this world record from Fred Bousquet. Cielo officially became the world's fastest 50-meter freestyler at the 2009 Brazil Open. He's also the most successful Brazilian swimmer in history, with three Olympic medals and six World Championship gold medals.

FASTEST FEMALE RUNNERS

Some runners seem unbeatable. Whether they're sprinting a short distance or pacing out a long run, they often make the sport seem effortless. The athletes listed here truly blew past the competition. Check out our list of the fastest times recorded by women running the 100-meter sprint.

10. and 9. (tie)
Ivet Lalova: 10.77 seconds
This Bulgarian sprinter *(left)* posted the above time in her home country in 2004. One year after that event, she broke her leg in a collision with another runner. After a long, slow recovery, she came back to win a gold medal in the 100-meter sprint at the 2012 European Championships.

Irina Privalova: 10.77 seconds
Russian athlete Privalova specializes in indoor running and currently holds the world indoor record for both the 50- and 60-meter sprints. She also has several Olympic medals to her name: a silver and a bronze from 1992 and a gold and a bronze from 2000. Between those Summer Games, she set this record for the 100-meter sprint at the 1994 European Championships.

8. and 7. (tie)
Veronica Campbell-Brown:
10.76 seconds

Specializing in the 100-meter and 200-meter sprints, this Jamaican sprinter is a champion in both categories. In four Olympic Games appearances (2000, 2004, 2008, and 2012), she's won seven medals. She set her personal best in the 100-meter in 2011. She's also one of only nine athletes ever to win world championships at the youth, junior, and senior levels of an event.

Evelyn Ashford:
10.76 seconds

This US runner was the first woman ever to break 11 seconds in the 100-meter sprint—which she did when she brought home the gold medal at the 1984 Olympics. Later that year, she set the 100-meter record, which held until Florence Griffith Joyner broke it in 1988. At Ashford's last Olympics, in 1992, she became the oldest American woman to take home an Olympic gold for track and field.

<<< 6. Kerron Stewart:
10.75 seconds

Even athletes at the top have to get used to coming in second. Jamaican sprinter Stewart won the silver medal in the women's 100-meter at both the 2008 Olympics and the 2009 World Athletics Championships. She also holds the women's record for the fastest nonwinning 100-meter time. This 10.75-second finish at the 2009 Worlds still put her behind Shelly-Ann Fraser, who won the race with 10.73.

5. Merlene Ottey: 10.74 seconds

Ottey, from Jamaica, has 14 World Championship medals under her belt—more than any other female sprinter in history! She's also competed at more Olympics than any other track-and-field runner. Her seven Olympics between 1980 and 2004 helped earn her the nickname Queen of the Track. So did this race time, which she clocked at the 1996 IAAF (International Association of Athletics Federations) Grand Prix Finals.

<<< 4. Christine Arron: 10.73 seconds

This French racer is the only European record holder on this list. Though she was born in Guadeloupe (a French-controlled island region in the Caribbean), she has lived in France since 1990. She ran her record-setting race at the 1998 European Athletics Championships. In 2004 she was part of the French Olympic team that won bronze in the 4×100-meter relay.

3. Shelly-Ann Fraser-Pryce: 10.70 seconds

When she was 21 years old—and unknown to most fans—this Jamaican sprinter captured the gold medal for the 100-meter dash at the 2008 Olympics. Four years later, she clocked the third-fastest 100-meter time in women's racing history at the Jamaican Olympic Trials. She then went on to bag a gold medal at the 2012 Olympics.

2. Carmelita Jeter: 10.64 seconds

This US runner became the second-fastest woman ever when she won the 100-meter at the Shanghai Golden Grand Prix in 2009. She also shines as a relay racer. At the 2012 Summer Games, she helped carry Team USA to a record-breaking victory in the 4×100 relay. (The previous record had stood for 27 years!) In all, she holds three medals from the 2012 Olympics, plus three more from World Championships.

1. Florence Griffith Joyner: 10.49 seconds

Known as Flo-Jo, this US runner became the fastest woman in the world when she posted this time at the 1988 Olympic Trials. She also holds the Olympic record for the same event—based on her 10.62-second win at the 1988 Summer Games. Not impressive enough for you? She also set the world record for the 200-meter sprint. Sadly, Griffith Joyner died of a seizure at the age of 38, in 1998.

Florence Griffith Joyner clocked a record-setting time for the 100-meter dash at the 1988 Olympics.

GREATEST NFL QUARTERBACKS

Quarterbacks need to be leaders. They must have strong and accurate arms. And they need to be smart enough to make split-second decisions. So what makes a truly great quarterback? It may be a combination of all these skills—and the results they produce. Here are the 10 NFL QBs with the most passing yards:

10. Drew Bledsoe: 44,611 career yards
Bledsoe was the star player for the New England Patriots in the 1990s. Of 14 NFL seasons, he spent nine with the Patriots (1993–2001), three with the Buffalo Bills (2002–2004), and two with the Dallas Cowboys (2005–2006). He was the youngest quarterback in NFL history to play in the Pro Bowl, at the age of 22.

9. Vinny Testaverde: 46,233 career yards
In 21 seasons, spanning the late 1980s to the 2000s, Testaverde played with seven teams: the Tampa Bay Buccaneers, the Cleveland Browns, the Baltimore Ravens, the New York Jets, the Dallas Cowboys, the New England Patriots, and the Carolina Panthers. Though he played in just 10 postseason games, his long career helped him secure his spot on this list, as well as No. 10 for career touchdown passes.

8. Fran Tarkenton: 47,003 career yards
Fran Tarkenton held the No. 1 spot on this list for nearly 20 years—from 1976 until 1995, when Dan Marino surpassed him. Tarkenton had a sandwich career, playing for the Minnesota Vikings on both ends (1961–1966 and 1972–1978) and the New York Giants in between (1967–1971).

7. Tom Brady: >>>>>> 49,178 career yards
Brady became the face of the New England Patriots in the 2000s. In his first 13 seasons as starting quarterback (2000–2001), Brady took his team to the Super Bowl five times and won three. He also led the Patriots to 10 division titles, another first for an NFL quarterback.

6. Warren Moon:
49,325 career yards

In his 17 seasons with the NFL (1984–2000), Moon played for the Houston Oilers, the Minnesota Vikings, the Seattle Seahawks, and the Kansas City Chiefs. He held records for most passing touchdowns, most pass completions, and most pass attempts—until Brett Favre broke all three records in 2007 and 2008. After leaving the field, Moon became a broadcaster for the Seahawks. He was inducted into the Hall of Fame in 2006.

5. Drew Brees: 51,081 career yards
Brees started his NFL career with the San Diego Chargers (2001–2005), but he's best known for wearing the uniform of the New Orleans Saints, where he's QB'd since 2006. In 2010, he led his team to a Super Bowl victory, not to mention a franchise record of 13 regular season wins.

4. John Elway: 51,475 career yards
Elway played for the Denver Broncos from 1983 to 1998, with a record five Super Bowl starts. He led the Broncos to their first-ever Super Bowl in 1987. The following year, he did it again. Elway retired from playing after the 1998 season. But he returned to the Broncos in 2011 as executive vice president of football operations.

3. Dan Marino: 61,361 career yards
In 17 seasons with the Miami Dolphins (1983–1999), Marino smashed dozens of records and led his team to 10 playoff appearances. His record for total passing yards in a single season—5,084 yards in 1984—stood until 2011. Even though he never won a Super Bowl, Marino is considered one of the greatest QBs of his era.

2. Peyton Manning: 64,964 career yards
Manning comes from an NFL family. His father is former quarterback Archie Manning, and his younger brother, Eli, is the New York Giants' starting quarterback. Peyton spent 14 seasons with the Indianapolis Colts before moving to the Denver Broncos in 2012. Both Fox Sports and *Sports Illustrated* named Peyton Manning their NFL Player of the Decade for the 2000s.

1. Brett Favre:
71, 838 career yards

In two decades as an NFL quarterback—most famously for the Green Bay Packers from 1992 to 2007—Favre lined up an impressive number of records. Those include the most passing yards, pass completions (6,300), starts by a player (298), and wins by a starting quarterback (186).

TRACKING
TOP TENS

When it comes to the biggest and the best in sports, we've barely scratched the surface. But now you know a little more about some of the world's top athletes. And you've seen what it takes to earn a spot among the top 10.

There are lots of ways to decide who's the "top." Is an athlete the best because she won the most medals or set a record time? Everybody may have a different answer to that question. So when you see a top 10 list, ask yourself, "What criteria did this list maker use?" Then you can decide if you agree with it.

You can also think about criteria when you make your own top 10 lists. We all like to give our opinions on what's best (or what's worst). When you put lists together using trustworthy criteria, your verdicts can stand up to the doubters. Turn the page to try your hand at creating lists of sports stats and stars.

Based on your criteria, Bjørn Dæhlie
may be the No. 1 Olympian of all time.
After all, he's won more Winter Olympics
medals than any other athlete!

Now that you've checked out our top 10 lists, it's time to make your own! First, think about your favorite sports. What impresses you the most about certain athletes? How can you measure their skills?

Come up with ideas for lists that spark your interest. Love baseball? What about highest batting averages? Smitten by horses? Try tracking the fastest steeplechase times.

Once you've got your idea for a list, it's time to do the research and find your Top Tens. Then add a few sentences about the facts you used to make your list. You might also want to add a few interesting facts about the people—or places, things, or events—on your list.

Try These Other Top 10 List Ideas

- Fastest downhill ski times

- Fastest NASCAR times

- Fastest slapshots in the NHL (National Hockey League)

- Most games won by a professional soccer team

- Most points scored in an NBA game

- Longest home runs in baseball

- Longest touchdowns in NFL history

- Highest-scoring gymnasts of all time

amateur: someone who does something as a hobby, not professionally

broadcaster: someone who describes or discusses something on TV or over radio

decorated: to have received medals or badges for accomplishments

dominate: to be the most influential, best, or most obvious part of something

era: a period of time, often linked to a specific event or person

executive: a person who has a senior job at a company

freestyle: a category of swim competitions where swimmers are allowed to choose from several types of strokes

philanthropist: a person who helps others by giving money or time to causes or charities

qualify: to reach a level or standard that allows you to do something

relay: a race among teams in which each team member completes a different part of the race

reunified: brought together again after a separation

roller skiing: cross-country skiing in a snowless area with long, ski-like inline skates

trials: contests to decide who qualifies for a larger or more important competition

NFL
http://www.nfl.com
You can watch games and other videos, read about your favorite players, and get all the details on stats and scores at the NFL's official website.

Olympics
http://www.olympic.org
Get the scoop about Summer or Winter Games—including athletes, medals, and events—at the official website of the Olympic Games.

Sports Illustrated Kids. *STATS! The Greatest Numbers in Sports.* New York: Time Home Entertainment, 2013.
Get the numbers on all your favorite sports, from baseball and football to golf, surfing, and car racing.

———. *1st and 10: Top 10 Lists of Everything in Football.* New York: Sports Illustrated Kids, 2011.
This book presents top 10 lists, trivia, and everything else you've always wanted to know about football.

Stewart, Mark, and Mike Kennedy. *Touchdown: The Power and Precision of Football's Perfect Play.* Minneapolis: Millbrook Press, 2010.
Go beyond the record books to explore all aspects of bringing the ball into the end zone.

WNBA
http://www.wnba.org
Learn more about WNBA players, teams, schedules, and statistics on the league's official site.

PHOTO ACKNOWLEDGMENTS

The images in this book are used with the permission of: © Mark J. Rebilas/USA TODAY Sports/Newscom, pp. 4–5; © Jed Jacobsohn/Allsport/Getty Images, p. 6; AP Photo, p. 7; © Focus on Sport/Getty Images, p. 8; © Al Bello/Getty Images, p. 9; © Christian Petersen/Getty Images, p. 10; © Phillip Peters/NewSport/CORBIS, p. 11; © Chuck Myers/MCT via Getty Images, p. 12; Harry Walker/KRT/Newscom, p. 13; © Mike Hewitt/Getty Images, p. 14; © Stephane Danna/AFP/Getty Images, p. 15; AP Photo/Eugene Hoshiko, p. 16; © Paulo Santos/Reuters/CORBIS, p. 17; © Johannes Eisele/AFP/Getty Images, p. 18; © Oliver Morin/AFP/Getty Images, p. 19; © Friedemann Vogel/Bongarts/Getty Images, p. 20; © Allsport UK/Allsport/Getty Images, p. 21; © Elsa/Getty Images, p. 22; © Vincent Laforet/Allsport/Getty Images, p. 23; Todd Kirkland/Icon SMI 488/Newscom, p. 24; © Jonathan Daniel/Getty Images, p. 25; © Clive Brunskill/Allsport/Getty Images, pp. 26–27.

Front cover: © iStockphoto.com/spxChrome; © iStockphoto.com/Bulent Ince (background).

Main body text set in News Gothic MT Std Condensed 12/14. Typeface provided by Monotype Typography.